Morgan

After your day of triumphs
you lay across my lap dozing.
I traced the line of your leg
with one finger
spare flesh and sinew
not enough surely to propel you
across the fields of your heaven.

How can those insubstantial limbs
underwrite all your rejoicing?
Do you hold proof that faith
is not a hopeless quest after all
that our faithful spirit can cut
the cord that tethers us
to the merely physical?

Death of a Children's Entertainer
On hearing of his death defending Ukraine, his home

He has vanished like so many others
torn apart by the Beasts of War
but I seem to see him reassemble
as if in one of his illusions.

Now pay attention children
as he turns all those shells and bombs
into coloured balloons pop-popping
high above your heads.

Stay under the big blue umbrella
that he conjured up for you.
Stay under his spell children.
Stay as long as you can.

The Cheviots

Nothing has really changed here
since the Romans looked northwards
to a land they would never conquer.
In all that time
these hills have never surrendered
they will tolerate only a few sheep
and the visitations of birds
who go where they will.
Even the road running through them
feels like an impertinence
to be shucked off at any time.

Dogs Enjoy the Morning

You make friends with your day
before I am out of bed.
No clouds invade your horizon.
You run to me grinning
eager to impart the good news
that this day is ours
and nothing is yet decided
and nothing is yet lost.

Out of Time
for C.K.

I don't remember taking the picture.
It must have been on some day out of time
when the Furies had forgotten
their business with you.

You look up smiling beatific
in that moment of peace
transfixed by some bird in flight
or perhaps a chink of blue sky.

Or just possibly you had caught sight
of some light of deliverance sent
to guide you through those sorrows
and bring you safely home.

Camster Settlement

Perhaps that little dog of yours
saw those that we could not
or heard their Ancient Voices
carried on the wind.
I saw him raise his head
and turn around
as if watching their hounds' approach
or waiting patiently
for the touch of curious children.
Did the men look up
from their butcher work
or the women from their milling
amused by this cheerful visitor
finding his world
in a blade of grass?
I think it was us
who were blind that day
for these villagers
must still be there living between
one breath of wind and another
a song in the cold air
or a murmur among the trees.
For why would they leave behind
all that they had made here?
A life fashioned with the sharpest flint.

The Luminous Roads of Spring

Spring's luminous road
was laid out before us
under blue sky and scudding clouds.
The season's strengthening light
amplified the bareness of skeletal trees
just as it poignantly tried to breathe
them back to life.
We travelled on together
the scent of last year's roses
long forgotten.
We scoured the trees along our way
each vying for the sight
of the first bud
assurance of yet another rebirth
that neither of us would admit
we had begun to doubt.

Mull

This place cradles the old stories well
and burnishes them with its own memory.
Watered with the sweat of generations
it has not always been generous.

This is not soft yielding Lowland
but a hard jewel set in changing waters
and to its hewers and toilers
always sparing with its gifts.

Owl's Flight

You carry the night on your wings lightly.
It does not bear down on you
as you glide through the velvet dark.
I envy you the instinct that carries you
through the empty black space
to your intended perch.
In my dark hours I am willing to believe
in a safe harbour for us all
reached by unquestioning faith
even on a starless night.

Old Men and Dogs

Old men and dogs enjoy the
morning
and see no reason to race to noon.
All hopeful things happen early.
All disappointment comes too soon.

Choral Evensong
Magdalen College

We exchange the noise and colour
of Oxford's Sunday streets
for the half-light of Magdalen Chapel
and discover once more
that a flickering candle
is proof against the deepest dark
as we wait to be immersed
in that centuries-old
river of worship
at one with all those
gone on before.
At one with the weak and the strong
all the rich and poor and all
the faithful and despairing.
This is worship
burnished by the Ages
so that when we return to
the busy night streets
those humble candles will continue
to light our way and proof us
against the swirling world
around us.

The Conversations
For Alison Ellen Smith

It is the only sane place.
The world that we convene
over coffee and cake
every now and then.

The jangle of the everyday
fades away and quiet voices
once again assert
their rightful authority.

And always this alchemy
transforms the everyday
and opens the door
to that other world.

The veil is torn away
and what was dancing
at memory's edge
comes to shine again.

We do not deal in
shadows.
Nothing has faded.
The sun is at its highest
in this particular sky.

The memory of small things
vouches for the reality
of all those greater wonders
that dazzle our eyes…

Your Mother's fabled soups.
Mine telling us at tea
of the books that she was reading.
Fathers and their foibles.

Those we love are not pinned
as butterflies under glass
but moving between two worlds
surely freer than us.

Time is irrelevant at this table
and death itself is forced
to loosen its grip on all we love
all that has gone before us.

And once again the old truth -
faith does not exist in a vacuum.
It is nurtured by those of others.

Edinburgh Echoes

They sing
around the Grass Market
and down the hill to Stockbridge
and through the Gardens
and everywhere I used to go.

Time's patina grows deeper
with forty years of memories
that stand like hard diamonds
on every corner.
Their brightness has no mercy.
It pierces the heart.

Late Afternoon

Winter. Late afternoon.
Walking home.
The dark is not yet complete
and the clouds are great
grey and purple bruises
a reproach perhaps for a world
only too able to create
its own darkness.
Before I reach my door
I look up once more
to see those lowering clouds
pushed aside
to give a glimpse of that place
beyond all fears.
There is still light enough
in this bruised sky
to encourage hope
light enough to let us believe
in the possibility of our Salvation.

Mc Arthur's Tea Room
St Andrews (1969)

He sat at his own table
in the dining room with the bay window
unchanged in decades.
According to the waitress
he had been a regular all that time.
She seemed proud of the fact.

He was there whenever we went
and always at the same table
a corporeal ghost bony frail
and with skin as thin as tissue.
He had lived a life of service
a Churchman much beloved.

I wondered who he would choose
to grace his table again? Wife parents
the Army friend who did not return. Once
I saw him staring ahead smiling
as if at last he had seen his Saviour
as if this business of loneliness
was at an end.

Garden Birds
(For my sister)

They flock to your generous table.
Blackbirds Starlings Finches Sparrows
all the tribes of the air.
We watch them fill their slight frames
and feel extravagantly pleased
with our charitable efforts
hoping that our alms sustain them
on whatever journey lies ahead.
If we see them as beggars or supplicants
how do they regard us?
Peering out from behind our window.

Soaring and tumbling joyfully
through the halls of their Heaven
do they pity us as we remain tethered
to a jealous world
that will not let us go?

Jack Kerouac - *On the Road*

You set out across the country with brother Neal*
and America came at you in a torrent
just as fame did later. Cities small towns farms
passed you both by in a heartbeat.
Stockyards diners deadbeat bars old men
staring down the road that had carried you and Neal
so far from the past.
Shining children all looking in the opposite direction.
Electric children all lit by the possibilities
offered by that bright continuing road.
It was all too much for you in the end.
The torrent blew you to the four winds.
You lost your anchor and when you reached
the other side of the Great Republic
you could only take refuge in half-lit bars
among the forgotten and the broken and the lost.
Your eyes were dazzled on that shining road.
You were blinded to the corporeal world
but you remembered everything everything
and this tumult swept you from the possibility
of wife children family life and that little world
bounded by a white picket fence.

*Neal Cassady, Kerouac's best friend, accompanied him on the
trip described in the novel, *On the Road*. Jack admired his ability to
have a family and provide for them.

Kyiv (2020)

What can we make of the Beast at the Gate
who looking beyond it can see no value
in those straight well-ordered streets?
Who bares his teeth at the sound
of honest speech and laughter
from all this shining city's cafes and bars.

What can we do to face down his snarling
and make his malice powerless impotent?
We can shine more brightly for each other
and speak more freely and laugh more loudly
so that the sound sends the beast howling
tumbling over a cliff of his own making.

Windfalls

We scoured the ground
for the fallen treasures
eager to gather in our prizes
before the season of bare trees
and unyielding ground.
They lay imperfect bruised
but there was still that
sweetness
locked inside.

A day later
we sat down to eat the pie
you had laboured over
as conscientiously
as in the days
when my enjoyment mattered
so much more to you.
Its warmth and sweetness
at odds with the chill
that hung in the air
between us.

Autumn Song
(For Hugh Mc Gee)

The last time I saw you
the leaves were falling all around.
Unconcerned with the ending of things
you looked heavenwards
and were rewarded
with the sight of light and colour
and swirling life
and somewhere just beyond
vouched safe by your faith
the bud of resurrection.

George Hornal

I come late with my gift
but it has multiplied
down grateful years.
Burnished every time
I remember you
holding friendly court
in that coffee house
as we "artists" sat
oblivious to the world
busy around us.

Your gift?
Admission to a table
where I spoke the same
language
as all the others there
where I learned that Art
comes before reward.
The threads you wove
into this tapestry
were imperishable.
They glitter still.

Among The Hills

Turning the car up into the hills
we found our moment out of time
and for a while the world below
stopped snapping at our heels.
There were small treasures
along our way.
Winter sun shining at an angle
through a small wood
a tidy hamlet almost too perfect.

You pointed to a house
with a neat garden and said
I can just see you living there
writing at your desk.
I was pleased with the thought.
But for my part I wished for
a compassionate bird
for your troubled sky
a creature of strength and grace
who could lift your cares
from your shoulders
and carry them high over that hill.

Hare

I imagine you sprinting
across fields
through undergrowth
and under hedges
always managing to escape
whatever pursued you
with that look of defiance,
burning in your eye.

Running under the stars
and under the sun
up over the wooded hill
and across the sleeping
Valley below.
And never ever stopping
as if you could run beyond
the edge of the world.

As if you could outrun
those snapping dogs
men with guns
and those that take
pleasure in your torment
and all the world
and all its malice
on and on and on
never tiring never failing.

On and on
towards that Safe Harbour
that never gets any nearer
but you continue tirelessly
as if you understand
that hope is its own refuge.

Northern Edge

(On the road between
Dunnet Head and John O'Groats)

Those dwellings stand together
a staunch army
guarding that storm-haunted coast
and shouting defiance
against the invader
that would devour the very earth
they stand upon.

Eyeless deserted cottages
cradle the memory of
long forgotten children.
Their silent stones record
the small victories
gouged from this stern land.

Those who came after
look out confidently through
their double-glazed windows
daring the great waters
to come and take
what they have made.

But the sea gives no hint
of surrender
no promise that these fields
will not someday
be part of its Kingdom
or the winding road to town
be lost forever.

And still the defenders
come in waves
generation after generation
laying its claim
and standing against that invader
that can never stop advancing.

The Curlew Road

At last after all those years
we found the Curlew Road.
Climbing from the valley below
escaping the tangle of the years
and claiming our prize
we found all the wonders
that the wild things know.
Amid the cry of Plover and Moorhen
and graced by Summer Winds
we noticed how the July sun
favoured certain distant hills
and knowing we could not stay
where we were for long
we set our course
for those bright holy places
with faith and glad hearts
remembering with gratitude
how we saw them first
from the Curlew Road.

Mr Proudfoot Finds Grace at Last

At last he made peace with Time
for it was Time itself that peeled away
one burden after another.
Ambition and all the old desires
were swept away as his sky cleared.
His faith grew stronger and brighter
as his limbs grew duller and weaker.
Movement was circumscribed by frailty
but there was no time for despair.
His world was simpler now
and light was everywhere.

Morgan at Kelso
(With love for Morgan and her Mistress)

Each time we let her off her leash
in those days of our Summer
she ran straight to her happiness
and found it every time.
There were no enemies
under her blue sky
and no prey whose blood
would taint the day
just the pleasure of running
and jumping headlong into the river
that would always support her joy.

And as we fretted about tomorrow
she chased her tail unconcerned
as if she knew the world was simpler
than fools like us could ever tell
and that the getting of happiness
was merely a matter
of running toward it.

One Day

One day
the tears of all the great clowns
will be wiped dry by the Mothers
who left them long ago.

One day
every step along the tangled path
that led to our lesser selves
shall be retraced.

And one day
that longed-for second chance
will appear on every street corner
given away with the Evening News.

Spring, Edinburgh New Town

The New Town is dreaming after the rain.
Its roofs and cobbles gleaming
it pretends all the dusty past is washed away.

The weight of history is great
but this Spring day has no patience
with the sullen army of yesterdays
as a sweet sudden breeze
sweeps away the last of Winter.

The world we shared comes rushing
in a torrent of Spring colours
that bring the scent of early flowers
and from a room
somewhere above my head
I hear you sing to me of love
and all the hopeful years to come.

Yachts

High above the town
gazing out to sea
I saw the yachts
drifting dreamily between
blue and blue
and just for a moment
I wondered what homecoming
would have been worth
leaving the dream behind.

The Mushroom Pickers

We were new to each other then
strangers who had strayed
into each other's country
edging towards a closer union.
Trust was a thing won by inches
and love waited eagerly
for its vindication.

We must do something
about those mushrooms you said
one lazy Autumn Sunday.
If we don't make a move
we'll miss our chance.
Ever tasted Chanterelles?
Absolutely wonderful!

Those Autumn woods
seemed to be waiting for you.
You set to work
with all your usual confidence.

You sure you know
what you are doing? I asked
much more than once.
I thought I saw you bridle
but you said nothing.

Envious of your expertise
I longed to earn my keep
and so I reached for something
that seemed to fit our purpose
but you steered my hand away
laughing and shaking your head
I was in YOUR hands then.

In the big dish on the kitchen table
our bounty looked for all the world
like trumpets eager for a fanfare.
You dusted each one reverently
treating them like fleshy jewels
you prepared them with an omelette
and a creamy sauce.

I couldn't describe the small wonders
that you laid before me.
You were a lady of unexpected gifts
that I could only receive
wide-eyed and dazzled.

In bed that night bound together
in the untroubled dark
you took that kind hand
and guided mine toward your breast
your heart in my hand
and mine singing in yours.
A union closer now.

The Memory Pearls

The necklace breaks.
The pearls scatter.
And somehow it is not enough
for her to know that
though lost for a while
they are still nearby.

She wants them all back.
The moments and memories
and those who made them.
She wants them all back.
Secured together and shining
before her dazzled eyes.

Tiger in the Rain

Week follows week.
Sterile years pile up and yet
he makes a good fist
of holding back The Furies.
But still they snap at his heels;
advancement refused at work
others' denial of his worth
ill-chosen words
that saw love flee.
The scent of lost Summers.

He holds them all in check
but then sometimes walking home
late at night when a shower of rain
has washed the world clean
and the stars look down
coldly illuminating the contours
of the life that he feels
he should be living now
rage assaults his broken heart.
On such nights his step quickens
and he prays that the rising wind
will blow away those torments
before he reaches his room
and a whisky and that recurring
late-night film that plays over
and over and over in his head.
All night and every day.

No Lesser Heaven
(For the young man sitting with his carer
at the next table)

Yours is no lesser heaven.
The stars will find you as surely
as they will find us all.
The sun will not withhold its warmth
just because you cannot
walk toward it.

True the paths you might have taken
are hidden by obscuring mists
but when that hour comes
and they melt away
you will find that nothing
lay behind them
that can outshine the New Glory
where all are made whole again.

Yours is no lesser heaven.
Wasn't it you that I saw
that day in The Gardens your gaze
fixed on the sky just above
those shimmering trees
as Summer swam in your eyes?

And I wondered with envy
why I could not see the Glory there
that shone so brightly for you.
Yours is no lesser heaen.

Mungo in Wykeham Forest

(For Mungo Otterburn,
good-hearted Hooligan)

You were rejoicing before we arrived
in the back of the car throat bared
you sang your hymn
to the place that sang to your soul.

You were impatient for the heaven
that embraced you in an instant.
Only the sound of partridges put to flight
vouched for your presence.

We discuss your character flaws
reckless headstrong and foolish
but we know there is no malice
in that giddy gambolling heart.

We can't imagine that the small lives
that you are ruffling now
are in any danger as you rush by
inebriated with your own happiness.

Then there is a silence that chills.
Nothing flutters among the trees
and there are no rustling leaves
on the forest floor.

Are you playing the old game
or has the very place you love
swallowed you whole or turned you
into a true restless running spirit?

We reassure ourselves
that you have done this before.
That's spaniels for you.
But this time the wait seems longer.

We look anxiously at each other
and retell all the possible scenarios
trying not to let our imaginations
conjure up greater horrors.

A dot appears far up the forest track.
You run back to us grinning sure
of the love that waits for you.
Heedless of a grief averted.

Anne Frank

For those of us who cannot
encompass the full horror
perhaps it comes down to this.
The silencing of one girl's voice.
The ending of her song
and the tearing up of the road
laid out for her.

Is this not a kind of blasphemy -
the appropriation of such power?

Once in The Anne Frank House
I heard a voice inappropriately loud
and for a moment,
wanted it silenced.

Autumn Winds

She thought it might have been
carrying the shopping home yesterday
or the fall last week.
More likely she assumed it was just
the wear and tear of years.

He moves the sponge down her back.
She flinches and he apologises as if
for every time he had ever let her down.
No. No she says it's working.
It's better now. Any chance of
a cup of tea?

At the door he turns to ask
if she would like a bite to eat
a sandwich maybe?
She has risen from her bath
and the years have fallen away
with the bath water.

She waggles her fingers smiling
and motioning for a towel.
He wraps it tightly around her.
Perhaps if he holds her close enough
and says an earnest prayer
time will forget its business with her.

Waiting for his wife in bed
he examines his great coarse hands
more used to farm work than tenderness
and is thankful that with them
he can ease her pain.

When she comes he reaches for her.
Autumn winds are stirring outside
speaking of an approaching chill
but he feels her breath on his cheek
as she beckons him back
once again to Summer's Fields.

Beachcomber

Each day he walks the beach
hoping for some treasure
from the great sea.
He lives in hope of some token
however small
from that life
he once thought dry and barren.
Some days he finds his reward;
a memory cast upon the shore
that illuminates some small triumph
or a moment when love
still swam in his orbit.
It is enough to warm his blood
enough to keep hope alive.
After all if that sea is endless
so perhaps are its gifts.

Mother

The pebble on the beach
and the wave
are good metaphors I think
for the wave alone
gives the pebble its form
returning time and again
to spend everything on the stone
which owing to its nature
can never adequately give thanks
for each gift
each act of forgiveness.

The People in the Other Rooms

That three-storey house
was my first home away
from my parents' house
dusty run down and imbued
with the taint of fading lives
it was a foreign country
not governed by my Mother's
dedication to a clean
and tidy world.

After work I faced the tyranny
of blank white paper
and would sometimes struggle
for all of thirty minutes
before admitting defeat
and turning to Radio Luxembourg
for comfort unwilling to admit
that I had not the ability
to fill that void.

I would hear the footsteps
of those from the other rooms
or catch sight of them
retreating behind a door
into their own lonely orbit
and still I did not understand
and still I thought of myself
as part of some superior world.

But when the burden
of blank paper overcame me
I was forced to open my eyes
and take notice of the lives
lived next door to mine
I could no longer hide behind
my own door
or the sound of the radio.

Those lives daily pulled me
from my self-imposed isolation
and showed me that sadness
was not just a fictional concept;
the elderly widow who moved
silently through her day
the married couple hashing over
their troubles in the kitchen
and always when I wanted
to make myself a sandwich.

And then there was the drunk
who sang out his despair into
the emptiness of his starless night.
In the years since those days
I have lived in all their rooms
at one time or another.

After Rain

Last night he dreamed
of the streets
after the rain had been.
In the morning he longed
for its scent in the air
as if in the hope
that life's confusions
could be washed away
with the dust.

Under a cloudless sky
he wondered how
he could flush that dust
from his soul
and the sourness
from his heart.

What heights of faith
would he have to scale
to bring on
such a downpour?

A Deer at Appin

Your beauty was without vanity.
Before I could capture it
you fled further into the woods
and became a creature
of light and shade
and like a fool
I chased one vanishing moment
after another
and always the lens too slow
to capture the fleeting splendour.
A rustle of leaves a cracked twig
a glint of sun between the green
and the Spirit of the Woods
laughed with you.
And still
I chase the fleeting denying
what experience has taught
that all that is held too tightly
is crushed
and being crushed is lost.

The Women Sang to Him
Before the End

Some said he was not a good man
a neglectful husband and a distant Father
but it seemed in that room sweetened
with song as if the world recognised
that he had always tried to do his best
as he saw fit and that all his failures
had been honest ones a result of
his quest for some greater virtue.

Halfway between waking and dreaming
he was sure this must be the case
for some of those singers had suffered
at the hands of those as careless as he
and yet still they sang to ease his heart.

Could it be this way for us all
at the last when hope seems redundant
the world accepts that we did as well
as circumstances and our natures allowed.
The women sang to him before the end.

Valley

We came upon it suddenly.
Blessed by April sun
it shocked us out of
Winter's grasp
but we had an appointment
over the hill.

Everything looked perfect
in this unfamiliar world
contented sheep grazed
on grass celestially lit.
Their shepherd walked
toward them
calling out for his flock.
Our hearts were pierced
but we had a meeting
over the hill.

A farmhouse and cottages
dotted around the valley floor
sang of order and contentment
perhaps sight of this place
was a gift not to be questioned.
We wanted to stop
but we had business
over the hill.

And now we cannot return
for that moment will not
but the memory of it
gives us hope of some
more permanent heaven
where The Shepherd
calls for us by name
and we have no need
to struggle over the hill.

Empty Skies

The Great Black Crow
hangs over his head
and shows no intention
of flying away.
Another drink or two
and he thinks that
it might be persuaded
to move to another
part of his sky.
His thoughts flutter
like epileptic wings
in an overfilled head
as they flit back and forth
and up and down
returning to his failures
over and over again
as if he were in some dead end
he cannot escape
always alighting on
old sorrows and guilt
and never at rest.

He would scream
if only he could
or at least try to explain
to those around him
why he had tried to fly
but was always tethered
to the ground
by the lead weight
of fear and anger
and his refusal to believe
that two and two
can sometimes make five.

He has another few drinks
and though they have
the desired effect
he curses himself for
once again shrinking back
once again avoiding battle.
When he leaves this place
the skies will be clear again
and the Black Crow gone
but that will only remind him
of his cowardice.

Tansy
(a country cat)

You come in from the velvet night
starry with secrets
and curl up by the fire
hugging those treasures close.

What wonders have you seen Tansy
in your travels through the night?
Do the Spirits of the Wood
whisper in your ear as you pass by?

Is that what makes you venture
deeper and deeper among the trees
where even the stars can't find you.
Do the spirits sing to you there?

You are smiling in your sleep Tansy
you have conquered your fears
among the wonders and the terrors.
We are humbled by your grace.

Feral

Once I was part of Creation a part
of all that made sense in the world.
It is not so now.
The world has tilted on its axis
spilling all that ever mattered
across the desert of my new existence
and even the fire that burns inside me
cannot protect me from the cold
as I wander these frosted fields
from farm to farm.

I turn compassion away
with the gaze of one fiery eye
and slash with razor claws
at any helping hand.
Every act of violence
twists the bitter blade
deeper into my own heart.
Scraps that never satisfy
punctuate my day
and fear drives me at night
to the cover of the Woods.

Then in the moment
before sleep takes me
I see the stars above the trees
and hope it is a sign
that I am not yet
beyond God's reach.

The Sailor Dreams

His boat slips out onto the coal black sea
surely a kindly star will light the way
he must scour the world for a worthy gift
before any hope of day.

All the treasures he can imagine
lie just beyond his sail
gold and silver and gems and silks
will surely see he does not fail.

But in the depth of night he wonders if
she'd value any gift that he could bring
perhaps what would stir her heart
he can only find within.

But the world inside is stranger
tangled and still without a chart
the wind whips the waves around him
he feels a chill grip his heart.

The night is endless his star is failing
he fears a never-ending quest
he fears that only ever in his dreaming
can he lay his head upon her breast.

This Easter Light

This Easter light illuminates.
It dissolves all fears
and penetrates the darkest corner
and the most shrivelled heart.
It tears the veil
that separates us from those
we love gone on before.
Death cannot stand in the face
of Light like that.
It places a ruby in our hand
bought with the blood
of our Saviour
and when darkness gathers
we open our hand and behold
our dazzling gift
and know again
all that we need to know
all that will ever matter.

Elliot Junction

The soul of Summer
lay down a dusty track
and over a railway crossing.
In memory a brass sun hung
over blue water
and the world beyond
that crossing
seemed dreamily limitless.
I wondered what lay over
the horizon and if the water
would bear my weight
but the day's pleasures
came with a frisson of fear.
I wanted my parents close
and for the world to keep
its distance for a while longer
and I wanted my Father's
strong arm
to continue supporting me
as I pretended to swim
away from the shore.

The Rescue Cat
(For Pasha)

What shape are your dreams
little cat?
Do they take the form
of the long grass that
shelters you when you are
unsure of your surroundings
or the world that beckons
beyond the window sill
or just that warm lap?
Do you go again
down those lonely streets
confronting the old cruelties
on every corner?
Triumphantly seeing them
slither away defeated
by that love newly settled
on your grateful heart.

Poem for Jane Haining
(Martyred at Auschwitz because she wouldn't abandon the children in her care)

The stars fell out of the sky
and if you could have done
you would have gathered them up
one by one
and stationed them once again
in their rightful quarters
and as before
their shining would have shamed
the darkness around them.
But instead they made you
sew stars into all those little
coats and dresses
forcing you to chain
all the bright and shimmering
to the dull clod
of a poisoned earth.
Then at the dying breath
of that great evil
just when hope
fragile as a Spring flower
broke ground
you were sucked into the maw
and in your presence
the darkness around you
was shamed into nothingness.

For Wolfgang Schrader

It is a joy to find a new friend
later in life
those evenings spent together
glass in hand
carry a deeper resonance then.
Our stories acquire a richness
that comes with experience
and the retelling of them
they glow like
the malts in our hand.
Then as the evening draws on
and the border between
one hour and another melts away
we like to think
that those we have loved
come to shine within the love
that we have always held for them.

George Mackay Brown
in an Edinburgh Bookshop

He seemed to waft in on the air
as though this man rooted in Orkney's soil
could only dream of visiting the City
and for all anyone around noticed
he might indeed have been dreaming.

Tall gangly hair swept back
in extravagant waves
a child's face describing adult melancholy
an innocent far from the reassurance
and protection of home.

He came to me with his query speaking softly
and respecting my ability to help.
I imagined having a coffee with him
and all he could teach this would-be poet
before our cups were drained.

He left too quietly. It did not seem right.
There should have been bells trumpets
a fanfare to admonish those who derided him
for not deserting the island that fed him
the place that gave him his world.

Evening Light

The old man was a distant relative
of my Father.
We'd pass his cottage
on our way through The Glen
to our favourite picnic spot.
The house was high up off the road
almost as if he had already started
to leave this world behind.

On our way home we'd see him
standing at his door pipe in hand
surveying the day's garden work
unconcerned by the fading light.
Told to put his affairs in order
thirty years ago Dad said marvelling.

A child still I imagined the old man
holding death back at his door
and wondered at the shining of the Angels
that saw him through his night.

D Day, Falling Man

I have seen him fall
time after time after time
in one documentary after another
in a few feet of grainy film
he gets no further than three feet
onto that bloody beach.

He had no chance to strike back
no chance to put even a mark
on the body of that great evil
but he has earned his place among
those who stood victorious
when that evil lay vanquished.

And still imprisoned in that few feet
of monochrome he falls again and again
reminding us of sacrifices still being made
and we hope against hope against hope
that someday he will escape this prison
when no more sacrifices are needed.

A Border Churchyard

We had not been sure of our way
on that sleepy summer afternoon.
Time had made us strangers
in a land of echoes.

Hawick slipped further behind us
as we drove up through wooded roads
onto that higher plane
of dozing fields and sun-blenched hills.

At some crossroads or another
we argued in a desultory fashion
before continuing on our way
in the wrong direction!

Later pulling in off the road
we tried to penetrate the fog of time.
We had known the place so well
now it seemed lost like a cheap pen.

One more try you said
grief for lost things written on your face.
One more turn and there it was
Chance or Faith rewarded?

We found their stones side by side
Tam and Jean and Bill and Bella.
But that glorious afternoon
mocked any grave's finality.

Those neighbours whose presence
had burnished our memories for years
would surely not be sleeping
on as fine a day as this.

The scent of living growing things
would not be denied by those we knew.
We felt them as near as our thoughts
and offered thankful prayers.

The thinnest of veils separated us
as we remembered those seasons shared
but all that was left to do
was leave their heaven undisturbed.

The Garden Was My Father's Art

The garden was my father's Art
uncircumscribed by painter's lines.
His studio lay under an evening sky.
He worked alone silently
without fuss or fanfare.

His artistry stretched beyond any frame.
I watched from a distance
as he tended his roses with what seemed
like all the reverence
due to some great and holy office.

In bed on drowsy Summer evenings
the world was bathed in the scent of roses
and I truly believed my father's garden
lay right next door to Heaven.
I thought him God's own gardener.

Backwater Dam

We are all still there
under that glistening surface
even when the wind scours the valley
and whips up the waters we remain.
The waters have sealed memory.

My Mother is taking a photo of us children
lined up against the whitewashed farm cottage.
We are wearing our serious faces
posterity demands nothing less
but we still do not feel the weight of Time
Childhood Summers have no need of THAT.

We play all afternoon until
heat and fatigue force us indoors
where Jess the farm wife has cold milk
for my sisters and me
and listens to our childish stories
as if they mattered.

Those waters are not to be resented
they are on our side
they guard that country jealously
and will not permit any invasion
of all those happy stations
nor the trampling of uncaring feet
across our memories.

My sisters and I wait patiently
at the farm road end
for sight of our Father's car
bringing him back from his business
in town and I know as I did then
he will find that once again Time
has not disturbed this little world.

Evensong

The day's journey ends
with candlelight and incense
and there too grace awaits.
Faith multiplied this way
melts the traveller's heart
so that one by one
its chambers are lit again
and life is returned
by grace
to that which was dead
and all the cold stations
on that wintry road
melt away behind him.

Also by John R. Nicoll

The Balloon Man in Edinburgh
(Comic Novella)

The Inconvenient Girl
(Tartan Noir thriller)

Mr Proudfoot at the Angel
(Haunting Novella)

Contact the Author

john2write51@gmail.com

———————————

Michael Terence
Publishing

www.mtp.agency

mtp.agency

@mtp_agency